The Jarrold Book of

The Countryside in Autumn

with text by **E. A. ELLIS**

Jarrold Colour Publications, Norwich

Soon after the corn has ripened and been gathered in, nights turn colder and in the first days of September we begin to sense the crispness and sweetness of approaching autumn. Stubbles may bring forth a wealth of poppies, corn marigolds and virgin sheets of mayweed, liberated briefly from the light-stealing canopy of crop plants, while road verges may be equally gay with an aftermath of summer blossoms; but streaks of gold and crimson in leaves and stems here and there give notice of change and decay. We scent ripe blackberries on sunny days and the dew-laden atmosphere at dusk and dawn carries an ever-increasing fragrance of damp earth, moss and dead leaves. The mellowing is gentle in the beginning, but round about the equinox we can expect a stirring interlude of gales and showers as cooling air-masses round the fringes of the Arctic meet the warmer vapours of the Atlantic and create major turbulence. Then, as days shorten and nights become longer and colder, swallows and other summer birds know they must soon depart. The migrants make full use of autumn's bounty before they go, filling and fattening themselves, some with insects, others with fruits and seeds, to provide a store of energy which will sustain them on their journeys to the far south. Similarly, animals preparing to hibernate feed with special zest, while creatures such as mice and squirrels gather stores of nuts, seeds and berries to eke out their winter foraging. Honey-bees work flowers whenever possible, while butterflies and moths due to spend the winter sleeping also imbibe nectar for as long as sunshine and warmth permit, making good use of late-blooming ivy in this way. Vegetation in the waterways dies down quickly with the reduction in solar energy, releasing a great deal of nitrogenous matter in decay. This in turn stimulates the development of numerous micro-organisms which provide food for slightly larger creatures such as swarms of small crustaceans. Later in the season, when leaves fall into streams from overhanging trees and bushes, they become coated with a variety of elegant little water-moulds which, with other scavengers such as water hog-lice, soon reduce them to skeletons. Under-water colonies of moss-animals (Bryozoa) and sponges decay, leaving seed-like bodies to lie in mud until the following spring, just as many aquatic insects deposit eggs before dying. Soon the flame of autumn spreads across the countryside, transforming the foliage of woods, hedgerows, moorlands and marshes alike in a splendour of gold, rust and purple. This glory may be brief in a very dry season when leaves are quickly shrivelled by strong winds, but in a rainy season the rich colours linger and glow with the moisture contributed by wetting. A succession of frosty nights hastens the process of cork formation by which deciduous trees cast their leaves, while moisture collecting on leaf-surfaces at night also hastens leaf-fall. Finally, it only takes a few gusty days to strip the boughs and carpet the ground thickly with leaves. In woods, this thick leaf-blanket conserves moisture like a mulch and helps the underlying soil to retain its rising warmth. Shortly before this fresh covering arrives, the more mature leaf-mould of the woods produces a great crop of toadstools. Most of these time the development of spore-bearing structures ahead of the smothering effect of the new leaf harvest and their efforts coincide with moistening by autumn rains and a lessening of the risk of drying out which they suffer in summer. There are also many microscopic fungi which are quick to exploit the residual sap in dying leaves and stems at this season, while sooty moulds mature even on the honeydew dropped by tree aphids on to the undergrowth. Autumn's wealth of berries not only helps to sustain many resident birds and mammals as winter approaches. It is welcomed by the host of migrants flocking in from northern Europe, driven to seek food and shelter in these islands as winter cold and darkness advance from the polar regions very swiftly once the equinox has passed. There is also an influx of marsh and water birds from the far north as lakes, rivers and mires become locked in the grip of ice. Sea-girt Britain enjoys a milder climate mainly through the influence of the Gulf Stream on the tidal waters streaming round its shores, so it has become a natural refuge of winter bird visitors since the last Ice Age retreated some 15,000 years ago. Some species, such as members of the thrush family and vast flocks of Continental starlings arrive early, while we welcome the wild geese and swans of Iceland, Spitzbergen and Siberia somewhat later in the autumn. Heavy rains at this season produce rapid flooding in lowlands, accentuated by the decay of clogging weeds in streams and rivers which allows upland waters to move speedily. Some rivers in spate erode their banks, spreading sand and gravel which can be colonised by strand vegetation in summer. Many marsh plants and trees such as the alder produce seeds adapted for dispersal by flood waters. Autumn showers also refresh the sandy soils of heaths and dunes, encouraging not only the growth of established mosses and lichens, but also enabling the seeds of many small annual plants to germinate. Various sand chickweeds, small forget-me-nots and other species classed as 'winter annuals' start life in autumn and are ready to flower early in spring before hot, dry weather returns to wither them. In this temperate region, midway between the extremes of a fast-chilling northern land mass and Mediterranean warmth, the prelude to winter has many pleasant aspects. Quite often we enjoy an Indian summer in October and the sting of frost comes only as we approach the shortest day of the year.

Hedgerows

There is usually an aftermath of growth along waysides in autumn. Road verges cut in summer produce a wealth of wild flowers in September, while in fields weeds flourish on stubbles and headlands, adding bright colour to the countryside until ploughing is begun. Gold and purple blossoms predominate, attracting late butterflies, bees, wasps and other insects. Grasshoppers chirp away until the first frosts bring their lives to an end. Numerous moths emerge and can be found visiting ivy bloom at night. Slugs and snails are still active, while countless spiders spread their webs everywhere and gossamer drifts across the fields. Seeds ripen in abundance on waste ground and in hedgerows, providing a harvest for nomadic flocks of finches, while berries welcome incoming bird migrants, and fungus-gnats enjoy their annual autumn feast.

1

1. LONG-TAILED FIELD MOUSE (*Apodemus sylvaticus*). These lively rodents emerge from their burrows at night, skipping about like miniature kangaroos as they collect seeds and berries. They store quantities of these in underground larders. They are easily distinguished from other species by their large ears and prominent, beady eyes. As cold weather approaches, some of them tend to enter out-buildings and houses where they raid stores of fruit and vegetables.

2

4

2. COMMON SHREW (*Sorex araneus*). Although a great many adult shrews die towards the end of summer, a few linger until October, often as refugees entering houses, while their territories in the undergrowth are occupied by young born earlier in the year. They hunt mainly for insects and small molluscs, but are also scavengers and eat a certain amount of vegetable matter. Their presence may often be detected by their shrill, high-pitched squeaking. Many are taken by owls patrolling lanes and fields at night.

3. KESTREL (*Falco tinnunculus*). This is our most familiar hawk in Britain's country-side nowadays and it can be recognised at once from its habit of hovering above the fields as it watches for small mammals, or even insects such as grasshoppers and beetles moving in the grass below. When excited, it calls 'kee-kee-kee' very readily. The male's head and tail are blue-grey. The resident population is swelled by the arrival of varying numbers of migrants from north-west Europe in autumn. Many frequent the coast at this season.

4. FIELDFARE (*Turdus pilaris*). Large numbers of these birds come to us from Europe's northern forest belt every autumn, crossing the North Sea to reach the eastern counties from late September onwards. They move about in flocks, raiding first the reddening berries of hawthorn and then most other wild fruits while supplies last. They are the largest and most aggressive of the thrushes and utter loud 'chacking' calls as they squabble for food on the bushes. When food is exhausted in the east, the flocks move to the west country and Ireland. They roost communally in rough grassland.

5. GOLDFINCH (*Carduelis carduelis*). After the breeding season these finches travel about the countryside in family parties and later in large flocks, feeding on seeds of thistles, knapweed, burdock and teasel. As the weather turns colder they resort to birch and alder, with siskins and redpolls.

6. SMALL TORTOISESHELL (*Aglais urticae*). These gay butterflies often flock to garden flowers such as michaelmas daisies in great numbers during September when the final brood appears from caterpillars which have fed on nettles. Presently most of them enter houses, hollow trees or caves, for hibernation.

7. CLOUDED YELLOW (*Colias crocea*). In most years some of these butterflies migrate from southern Europe to reach England, where they produce one or more further broods from caterpillars feeding on lucerne and clover. Late-hatched specimens may be seen in early autumn, chiefly in the south and east.

8. RED ADMIRAL (*Vanessa atalanta*). **AT IVY BLOOM.** The first red admirals usually reach this country as migrants from the Mediterranean in spring. Two local broods follow, from caterpillars feeding on nettles. Very large numbers may turn up in autumn and some of these undertake a return migration southwards.

6

7

8

9. CATERPILLAR OF ELEPHANT HAWK-MOTH (*Deilephila elpenor*).

These large caterpillars with false 'eyes' and retractable 'trunks' have a somewhat alarming appearance when found crawling over the ground in early autumn as they prepare to dig themselves in and become torpedo-shaped chrysalids. They have fed earlier on willowherbs, bedstraws, balsams and cultivated fuchsias. The vividly coloured pink and green moths fly in July and August.

10. SILVER-Y MOTH (*Plusia gamma*).

In some years countless numbers of these greyish moths swarm over the countryside in autumn, visiting all sorts of flowers by day as well as night. They are the most prominent of all migrant moths invading us from the Mediterranean region, where breeding is continuous throughout the year. The caterpillars feed on a variety of wild and cultivated plants and are sometimes agricultural pests.

11. SCENTLESS MAYWEED (*Tripleurospermum inodorum*).

This is the commonest of all mayweeds thriving on fields and in waste places all over Britain and it grows on most types of soil. It continues flowering until well into the autumn. Although the daisy-like blooms are visited by many insects, including bees, cross-pollination is not needed for the production of seeds. The white ray-flowers are sometimes speckled with a brown downy mildew.

12. DARK MULLEIN (*Verbascum nigrum*).

Found fairly commonly in the southern half of England, this late-flowering mullein appears chiefly along roadsides and railways where there is chalk or limestone in the soil. Unlike most other mulleins, this species lacks extreme woolliness, its leaves being dark green and somewhat shiny above, with some starry hairs underneath. The flowers, which have velvety purple centres, yield a yellow hair-dye.

13. YELLOW TOADFLAX (*Linaria vulgaris*).

This attractive plant often produces a brilliant show of blossoms in autumn, following summer hedge-trimming. Bearing a close resemblance to antirrhinums, the flowers are specially attractive to bees and are succeeded by plump capsules packed with dry, winged seeds. Country names for this species include 'butter-and-eggs', 'rabbits', 'lion's-mouth' and 'brideweed'.

12

14. LEAVES OF BLACKBERRY WITH PURPLE-STAINING RUST FUNGUS (*Phragmidium violaceum*). As blackberries ripen in autumn some are taken by birds, field mice and foxes and those that are left are commonly welcomed as juicy food by wasps, fruit-flies and harvestmen. Finally, when over-ripe, they are consumed by various yeasts and moulds. At the same time the leaves often turn purple and crimson through blotching by special rust fungi.

15. BLACK AND GOLDEN BLACKBERRIES (*Rubus fruticosus* agg.). Almost 400 British micro-species of blackberry are distinguished by botanists, and even the observant amateur picking fruits along the hedgerows soon notices much variation in foliage, prickliness and type of berry met with. There are also early and late varieties and some specialising in particular habitats. One rare form bears yellow berries; another has double flowers.

16. LORDS AND LADIES (*Arum maculatum*). The shining scarlet berries of wild arum ripen after the broad, arrow-shaped leaves have died down completely in summer. They become conspicuous along shady hedgerows for a time, but are soon taken by birds once they have attained their full colour and become soft. Children must be warned not to eat them, since they contain poisons, including one similar to that found in hemlock. Fortunately they also have an unpleasant taste, which is a deterrent.

17. BLACK BRYONY (*Tamus communis*). The berries of this species festoon the hedges with trailing garlands of red berries, translucent and shining like jewels and surviving until quite late in the autumn, while the heart-shaped leaves turn yellow and wither, leaving them fully exposed to the view of passing birds which may be tempted to take them. These fruits have irritant needle-like crystals and narcotic juices which can cause vomiting and paralysis if eaten by children.

18. ELDER (*Sambucus nigra*). Elder-berries ripen in September and are raided very soon by blackbirds and starlings, so those who wish to gather them for making elder wine have to be early in the field. Among other competitors for these small but very juicy berries are robins and black-caps. There is a variety of the common elder which bears pale honey-coloured fruits which have a mild, sweet taste, but are neglected by birds.

19. WHITE BRYONY (*Bryonia dioica*). This common hedge-climber, which bears male and female flowers on separate plants, is the only wild member of the marrow family in Britain. It is a perennial, developing large, parsnip-like roots which are mistakenly called 'mandrakes'. The spherical berries, which are highly poisonous, ripen a dull red after the leaves have withered and are accompanied by conspicuous spring-like tendrils.

20. HAWTHORN (*Crataegus monogyna*). Our quickthorn hedges planted extensively in the eighteenth and early nineteenth centuries, when vast areas of common land were enclosed for cultivation, have featured prominently in the English countryside ever since, giving us the beauty of may-blossom and a wealth of crimson haws ripening in autumn. The bushes also grow naturally in the pioneer scrub of old grasslands. The berries are much eaten by fieldfares, redwings, blackbirds and other thrushes.

21. COMMON BARBERRY (*Berberis vulgaris*). This spiny shrub was once widespread in our hedgerows, especially in the eastern counties, but is now uncommon. Its present scarcity is due largely to the rigour with which it was destroyed throughout the country early in the nineteenth century when it was shown to be a carrier of the notorious black rust of wheat which then ravaged our crops. Since then it has been found that the rust is commonly able to persist without its aid.

22. BLACKTHORN (*Prunus spinosa*). This fiercely prickly shrub forms impenetrable thickets on derelict grassland and proves an effective barrier where it is planted in hedges. The snow-white blossoms appearing on leafless boughs in April are succeeded in autumn by blue-black sloes. These astringent fruits have a powdery 'bloom' on their skins; they ripen fully by early October and are then gathered for making sloe gin, mainly in southern England.

23. WOODY NIGHTSHADE or BITTERSWEET (*Solanum dulcamara*). Commonly mistaken for deadly nightshade, this perennial climbing plant bears clusters of attractive star-flowers with violet petals and spiky yellow centres during the summer. The berries have a bitter-sweet taste and contain the alkaloid poison solanine.

24. DEADLY NIGHTSHADE (*Atropa belladonna*). This is a large bushy perennial of limy soils, distinguished from other nightshades by the dull-purple, bell-shaped flowers. The solitary, very glossy black berries, resembling cherries, contain the virulent poison hyoscyamine; eating a single fruit can prove fatal.

25

26

25. OLD MAN'S BEARD or TRAVELLER'S JOY (*Clematis vitalba*). The presence of this climber in hedgerows is a sure indication of lime in the soil. The vines are supported by twisted, tendril-like leaf-stalks and are sometimes used in basket-making. The bearded fruits are conspicuous in autumn.

26. BUSH-CHEEP (*Pholidoptera griseoaptera*). This dark-brown bush-cricket frequents hedgerows almost everywhere in the southern parts of England. It clambers over vegetation on spidery legs mainly by night, feeding on insects, snails and fruits. Its chirping in the dusk only ceases when autumn frosts intervene.

27. COMMON WASPS (*Vespula vulgaris*) **ON APPLE.** Wasps are notoriously fond of sweet substances and are attracted by ripe fruits of many kinds, although they also catch flies to feed to their grubs. In damaging apples and plums they make things worse by spreading the moulds responsible for brown rot.

28. SECTION OF COMMON WASPS NEST. Wasps build their nests of papery material fashioned from pulped wood-scrapings. Inside, there are tiers of comb consisting wholly of brood cells, as no honey is stored. The nests are abandoned and decay when activity ceases at the approach of winter.

29. PARASOL (*Lepiota procera*). This tall, scaly toadstool with white gills and a movable ring on its stem appears commonly on road verges and park-land in late summer and autumn. It is one of our good edible fungi, with a delicate, sweetish flavour, but should not be eaten raw.

30. SEVEN-SPOT LADYBIRD (*Coccinella 7 punctata*). Sometimes called 'bishy-barnabees', these insects are very useful in destroying great numbers of greenfly in spring and summer. The adults commonly hibernate in hedges and are able to survive long exposure to frost and rain, being waxy and well weather-proofed.

31. LAWYER'S WIG (*Coprinus comatus*). The largest and most conspicuous of the numerous tribe of ink-caps, this fungus abounds on rubbish tips and well-manured pastures, especially during mild, showery weather in autumn. Its shaggy white or pinkish caps are good to eat, but soon turn black and dissolve.

32. ERGOTS OF *Claviceps purpurea* **ON RYE.** The horn-like sclerotia of this fungus parasitise the ears of most wild grasses as well as cereals. They contain several very poisonous substances which can cause gangrene, abortion and madness in people who eat bread made from diseased rye. This was the cause of the terrible scourge known as 'St Anthony's Fire' which affected great numbers of people from time to time in the Middle Ages.

Waterways and Marshes

The vegetation of open water decays rapidly in early autumn, releasing nutrients which become available for microscopic life then able to flourish while waters are clear in winter. Pond snails and some aquatic insects hibernate; others die in autumn, leaving eggs or larvae. Frogs submerge themselves in mud and fish seek deep waters to escape freezing. In marshes there are still many flowers brightening the scene through September, notably angelica, yellow fleabane and the amethyst 'pincushions' of devil's-bit scabious. Then the rank vegetation of damp places sheds its foliage, streaked with gold and touches of crimson here and there, until it becomes bleached or a withered brown. Reeds do not lose their leaves until very late in the autumn, to stand as bare canes topped with fluffy seeds through the winter.

33. BEARDED TIT (*Panurus biarmicus*). Long known to Norfolk marshmen as the 'reed pheasant', this species used to nest only in reed and sedge beds bordering the East Anglian rivers and broads. Although almost exterminated by the severe winter of 1947, it has since multiplied and spread to many new haunts. Nomadic flocks travel widely over the English countryside in autumn and winter, uttering metallic 'chinking' calls as they flit about the reed-tops.

34. REED BUNTING (*Emberiza schoeniclus*). The cock bird is readily identified by its black head and bib. The hen has streaky brown plumage rather like a sparrow. These birds nest low among tufted grassy vegetation in marshes, but many move away from wet places to forage along hedgerows and even on waste patches in towns as winter approaches. They flick their tails and usually utter querulous seeping calls as they move about.

35. PIED WAGTAIL (*Motacilla alba yarrellii*). Also called 'penny wagtail' and 'dish-washer', this is very much a bird of farmsteads and can be seen at all seasons. It is attracted by water and often appears to take a great interest in its reflected image in windows and the shiny bonnets of cars. The plumage is greyer over all in winter. It runs about in pursuit of insects, twittering and forever bobbing its long tail. Small seeds form part of its diet in autumn.

36. CENTRE-BARRED SALLOW MOTH (*Atethmia centrago*). This moth is associated with ash trees on which its striped caterpillars feed in early summer. It is one of the many plump-bodied moths attracted by lights at night in early autumn. When resting by day it is recognisable by the broad purplish-red band across the middle of its orange-yellow wings. At this season it is one of the numerous moths found on newly open flowers of ivy, which abound in nectar.

37. HERALD MOTH (*Scoliopteryx libatrix*). When at rest, this species resembles a withered leaf, complete with pale veining and jagged edges, while touches of rusty orange provide additional camouflage at a time when similar fiery tints are creeping into foliage everywhere. The grey caterpillars feed on willows and the moths are active for a month or two in autumn, after which they hibernate and reappear as pussy willows come into bloom in spring, enticing them to their nectar, as does ivy bloom in autumn.

38. COMMON REED (*Phragmites communis*). Our tallest native grass, sometimes eleven feet high, grows in thick beds by the waterside. After the leaves have been shed in autumn the stems are cut for thatching buildings.

39. DEVIL'S-BIT SCABIOUS (*Succisa pratensis*). The blossoms of this species appear in rushy places mainly in September. They attract many insects to their nectar, including the 'swing-winged' hover-flies shown here.

40. MARSH FLEABANE (*Pulicaria vulgaris*). This late-flowering species grows chiefly on clayey meadows. The leaves are felted and have a cat-like scent. A smouldering bunch of flea-bane is said to asphyxiate fleas.

41. MARSH ANGELICA (*Angelica sylvestris*). This is the latest of all our umbelliferous plants to come into bloom. Its white or faintly purplish flowers yield free nectar for a vast range of insects, from the smallest flies and beetles to bumblebees and butterflies. Later in the autumn its corky-winged fruits ripen and are dispersed by winds and floods.

42. YELLOW FLAG (*Iris pseudacorus*). These brilliant yellow irises with stiff, light-green sword-leaves flower profusely on open marshland in June. In autumn their fleshy pods ripen, splitting into three boat-shaped segments which scatter rows of bay-brown seeds. These litter the ground, waiting to be transported to virgin areas of muddy soil by winter floods.

43. WATER FERN (*Azolla filiculoides*). This miniature floating fern is to be seen chiefly on the surfaces of ditches and pools in East Anglia. Its fronds are at first pale green and sparkling with tiny beads of moisture, but turn red in autumn. Once prevalent as a native in Europe, it died out half a million years ago, but survived in North America, from whence it has been reintroduced in this century. Severe flooding has helped it to spread to new areas.

42

43

44

44. ROYAL FERN (*Osmunda regalis*). This is the largest of our native ferns, growing to about a man's height in the shade of alder swamps and sometimes in more open, boggy situations. Its spores are produced on separate spikes instead of on the backs of the leafy fronds in late May and June and for this reason it is known as the 'flowering' fern. The foliage turns yellow and then a brilliant orange rust colour in autumn. It will only colonise acid peat.

45. GUELDER ROSE (*Viburnum opulus*). Known anciently as the 'marrish elder', this shrub is closely related to common elder. It flourishes in moist situations where lime is present. It bears creamy white, night-scented blossoms in June and these produce umbels of shining, juicy berries which are attractive to birds of the thrush tribe and visiting waxwings in autumn. The bitter fruits are normally scarlet, but may be orange-coloured or crimson.

46. COMMON BUCKTHORN (*Rhamnus catharticus*). This prickly deciduous shrub, distinguished from alder buckthorn by its saw-toothed leaves, thrives on chalky ground and in non-acid marshlands. The small, yellow-green male and female flowers grow on separate bushes in June. The black berries ripen in autumn, but are inedible because of their strongly purgative action. The leaves are eaten by caterpillars of the brimstone butterfly. The wood of both buckthorns produces a super-fine charcoal.

45

47. GUELDER ROSE (*Viburnum opulus*). The leaves of this shrub turn a fiery red or crimson quite early in the autumn, often two months before they drop. The bushes stand out like beacons in the midst of other vegetation and it is possible that they help to attract birds as the berries are ripening, especially in misty weather when the red colour acts rather like the glow of a fog-lamp and is therefore visible from a distance. The bushes look specially beautiful mirrored in pools.

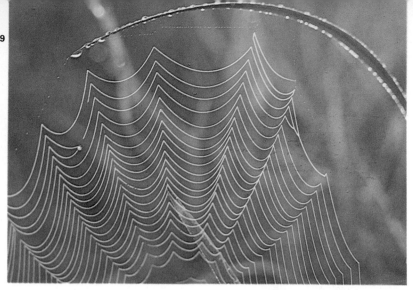

48. WILD PRIVET (*Ligustrum vulgare*). This straggling shrub abounds in marshy thickets and on chalk. Unlike the cultivated privet of garden hedges it sheds its leaves in winter. The heavily scented flowers are very attractive to butterflies in August; the berries, which are purging, ripen in October.

49. WEB OF DIADEM SPIDER (*Araneus diadematus*). The wide-ranging diadem spider, familiar in gardens, grows plump towards the end of its life in autumn and it is then that its beautiful geometric webs become most conspicuous, glittering with beadlets of dew early in the morning.

50. COMMON DARTER DRAGONFLY (*Sympetrum striolatum*). This medium-sized dragonfly often ranges far from its breeding-haunts in ponds and ditches in late summer and autumn, hawking insects and, at intervals, sunning itself on garden paths and bushes. While the females are olive-brown, the males become red.

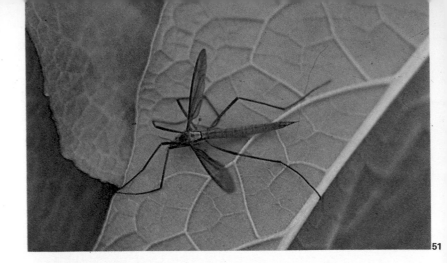

51. CRANE-FLY (*Tipula paludosa*). Immense numbers of these insects, commonly called 'daddy long-legs', emerge from damp grassland and drift clumsily over the countryside in early autumn, providing food for insectivorous birds. Their grubs, known as 'leather-jackets', are very destructive to grass roots.

52. LILAC MILK-CAP (*Lactarius lilacinus*). Only a few of the larger fleshy toad-stools are able to thrive in wet habitats. This rare species can be found occasionally under alders in marsh woodland. Its rosy lilac cap and yellowish gills yield a white, faintly acrid milk when bruised.

Coast

On the slopes of rocky cliffs, sea pinks, campions, blue sheep's-bit and autumn squills give lingering touches of colour in September. Along shingly beaches, horned poppies, sea kale and other strand plants run to seed. While the wind-whipped marrams bleach on the dunes, the moister nights of autumn refresh mats of moss and lichen in the hollows and sand fungi appear. The vegetation of mudflats and saltings dies away, suffused with sunset tints for a while. Birds leaving for warmer lands and others arriving for the winter commonly hug the coastline during their autumn passage migration. They include streams of sea birds moving off-shore. Many finches arrive to feed on the seeds of cliff and dune plants and even kingfishers often move to the seaside for a spell in autumn. Many seedlings of chickweeds and other 'winter annuals' sprout from dune sands.

53. DUNLIN (*Calidris alpina*). This is the most abundant of the many waders flocking to feed on our coastal mudflats. The greatest numbers gather in autumn and winter with the arrival of visitors from northern breeding grounds. As the birds circle and swerve in flight they appear shadowy and like shimmering snowflakes in turn, trilling as they go. They patter over the mud, probing its surface methodically for ragworms, crustaceans and small molluscs.

54. WIGEON (*Anas penelope*). As wintry conditions develop over the wetlands of northern Europe, great numbers of these whistling ducks take refuge here and flocks numbering thousands often gather on our tidal waters. They rest by day and feed on various types of grassy vegetation in estuaries at night.

55. LESSER WHITE-FRONTED GEESE (*Anser erythropus*). Several kinds of wild geese arrive in Britain from northern breeding territories at the approach of winter, notably brent, pink-footed and white-fronted. The lesser white-front is one of the rarer and more irregular visitors coming from Siberia.

56. SEA HOLLY (*Eryngium maritimum*) **WITH MALE COMMON BLUE BUTTER-FLY** (*Polyommatus icarus*). Silver-green, prickly sea holly grows on freshly formed sand dunes and its blue, thistle-like flowers continue to attract bees and butterflies for a while in September. The bleached foliage stands through the winter.

57. SEA ASTER (*Aster tripolium*). This wild michaelmas daisy with thick, tongue-shaped leaves grows in muddy salt-marshes flooded regularly by the tides. It blooms in August and September, afterwards producing heads of white, downy fruits, very conspicuous round the shores of estuaries in late autumn.

59

60

58. ALEXANDERS (*Smyrnium olusatrum*). Monks cultivated this yellow-green umbellifer in the Middle Ages, blanching the crowns like celery, boiling the leaves as a vegetable and putting the aromatic black seeds into soups. It now flourishes near the coast, where its seeding umbels are conspicuous in autumn.

59. PROSTRATE MARSH SAMPHIRE (*Salicornia ramosissima*). Several kinds of marsh samphire or glasswort mature in late summer and autumn on mudflats and salt-marshes. One bright-green, succulent species is gathered for pickling. They were formerly harvested and burnt to produce soda-ash for glass-making.

60. STAR CUP (*Peziza ammophila*). As sand dunes gather moisture in autumn, several special fungi develop from the remains of buried vegetation. This fleshy cup-fungus appears round clumps of marram grass. It has a rooting, stem-like base and its cups expand above in starry lobes.

61

61. DUNE STINK-HORN (*Phallus hadriani*). Unlike the common stink-horn of woodlands, this species sprouting from marram-clad sandhills in autumn has the sweet fragrance of hyacinths. It grows from violet-tinted 'eggs' and the dark, slimy spores on its cap are removed by carrion-flies.

Woodlands

Most of the undergrowth in woodlands, subdued by summer shade, dies down long before the approach of autumn. September showers bring forth troops of elegant toadstools whose mycelium has been accumulating nourishment from rotted leaf-litter under the trees. These fungi emerge to shed their spores before they become buried under a carpet of fresh leaves shed by deciduous trees as the season advances. There are numerous beetles and flies which feed on this bounteous fungus crop. As tree foliage turns russet and gold, ripe acorns and other nuts provide food in abundance for woodland birds and rodents, some of which lay up stores of them for the winter. Finally, as trees become bare and the nights turn cold, hedgehogs, dormice and many smaller woodland creatures including moths, bugs and beetles go into hibernation.

62. BURNHAM BEECHES, BUCKINGHAMSHIRE. Our most glorious beech forests have developed on chalk land since the climate of Britain became mild enough for these trees about 3,000 years ago. The famous Burnham beeches are somewhat exceptional in growing on sand and gravel, with patches of heathland. Many of the trees have crooked trunks, and some of the older ones with very thick boles and low, spreading boughs have been pollarded in the past.

63. FALLOW DEER (*Dama dama*). These dappled deer roam many English parks, having been introduced for hunting. They mate in autumn and the fawns are born in midsummer. The bucks shed their antlers in spring.

64. YOUNG ROE DEER (*Capreolus capreolus*). Baby roe deer are known as 'kids' and at first tend to have dappled coats. They may be born at any time between early May and the end of June.

65. ROEBUCK (*Capreolus capreolus*). Our native roe are small, standing less than a yard high. They seldom collect in large numbers. Ring-like tracks are made during the ritual of courtship. Bucks shed their antlers in March.

66. BADGER (*Meles meles*). Badgers range over most parts of Britain where woods and grassland are intermixed, but often remain unobserved, since they sleep by day in underground homes known as 'sets'. These hideouts are commonly in woodland and consist of several tunnels leading to chambers thickly bedded with dry leaves, moss and bracken. The animals emerge at night to sniff and root about in the undergrowth for slugs, snails, earthworms, wasp grubs, beetles and various small mammals (especially young ones in their nests). They grow fat in autumn and this helps them to survive hard winters.

67. GREEN WOODPECKER (*Picus viridis*). The laughing cry of the 'yaffle' or 'rain-bird' is heard most commonly when wet weather is approaching, possibly because this improves the prospect of digging out insects from the ground.

68. CHAFFINCH (*Fringilla coelebs*). Cock and hen chaffinches tend to gather in separate flocks during the autumn, when they spend much of their time pecking about under trees, especially when beech and hornbeam seeds abound.

69. WOODCOCK (*Scolopax rusticola*). Many of these birds arrive from northern Europe in autumn to seek winter lodging in our woods. They probe the ground for worms and grubs at night and skulk under cover by day.

70. RED UNDERWING (*Catocala nupta*). These large moths appear commonly in early autumn, resting by day on walls and tree trunks. The closed wings provide good camouflage, being grey and mottled like bark; they also resemble heads of lizards, complete with 'eyes'. On being disturbed, they produce a startling effect as the bright red-and-black lower wings are exposed.

71. CATERPILLAR OF PALE TUSSOCK MOTH (*Dasychira pudibunda*). Greyish-white tussock moths flying in May and June produce a late summer and autumn brood of elegant caterpillars which can be found feeding on the leaves of many kinds of trees, including oak, beech, birch, hazel and apple. They eventually pupate in cocoons of yellow silk.

72. MERVEILLE DU JOUR (*Dichonia aprilina*). This beautiful moth is coloured and speckled like some of the lichens of tree trunks, and although common in oak woods in autumn it is not often noticed, because of this protective camouflage. The caterpillars are greenish grey, with light and dark markings. They feed on oak leaves, but rest on bark by day.

73. ROWAN or MOUNTAIN ASH (*Sorbus aucuparia*). Rowans flourish notably in the Scottish Highlands, but are also common on many tracts of sandy country in England. Their berries ripen in August and September and are among the first to be taken by thrushes and blackbirds. These fruits have an astringent taste, but are sometimes made into jelly for eating with meats.

74

75

74. HAZEL NUTS (*Corylus avellana*). Hazel abounds mainly as an under-shrub in oak and ash woods. The nuts ripen and are shed as the leaves turn yellow in mid-autumn. The crop varies with the severity of the previous winter which affects the chances of the flowers setting properly.

75. ACORNS OF COMMON OAK (*Quercus robur*). May frosts can spoil the chances of a good acorn crop being produced in the following autumn, though such failures are rare. Acorns provide food for many creatures, including wood mice, squirrels, pheasants, wood pigeons, rooks, jays and woodpeckers.

76. SWEET CHESTNUTS (*Castanea sativa*). Believed to have been introduced by the Romans, the 'Spanish' chestnut is now widely naturalised here and often produces heavy crops in our southern counties, although the nuts are not so large as those imported from the south of Europe for roasting at Christmas.

77. HORSE CHESTNUTS (*Aesculus hippocastanum*). The now widely planted horse chestnut was introduced here in the seventeenth century. Its hard, shiny nuts, known as 'conkers', drop early in the autumn. Their skins are poisonous and they are inedible. The leaves turn a rich yellow and finally rusty on falling.

78. FRUITS OF SYCAMORE (*Acer pseudoplatanus*). Sycamore 'keys" can be seen hanging in green bunches quite early in summer, but do not ripen until autumn, when they turn pinkish and finally light brown before being whisked away by the wind, twizzling like propeller-blades in flight.

79. GREEN 'ISLANDS' OF CHLOROPHYLL IN DEAD OAK LEAVES. Various small insect grubs form tunnel-like pockets between the upper and lower skins of leaves. As they feed, their waste products accumulate and in autumn, when the leaves wither and fall, these keep some patches of green cells alive.

80. SPANGLE GALLS ON OAK LEAVES. All of these represent the unisexual generation of insects which produce quite different galls in spring. Top to bottom: silk button spangle (*Neuroterus numismalis*), common spangle (*N. quercus-baccarum*), smooth spangle (*N. quercus-baccarum*). They fall in autumn.

81. CHERRY GALLS (*Cynips quercus folii*). These mature on the undersides of oak leaves in autumn. Self-fertile female gall-wasps emerging from them lay eggs in dormant buds of oak and these produce violet-coloured, egg-shaped galls of the bi-sexual generation in spring.

82

82. DEATH-CAP (*Amanita phalloides*). This fungus of beech and oak woods is sometimes confused with mushrooms and the results of eating it are usually fatal. It can be recognised by its white (never purplish) gills, slimy, olive-streaked and faintly yellowish cap and unpleasant odour.

83. GREAT SPOTTED SLUG (*Limax maximus*) **EATING BLUSHER** (*Amanita rubescens*). Many toadstools are devoured by slugs at night, the molluscs being attracted by special odours so that they may act as agents for dispersing spores. Even the most poisonous fungi are eaten without the slugs suffering any ill effects.

84. HONEY-TUFT (*Armillaria mellea*). Clumps of this fungus sprout very commonly from buried tree-stumps in autumn. This species has mycelium which spreads underground to attack the roots and trunks of most kinds of trees, killing them. Affected trees have black, bootlace-like strands under the bark.

85. SCARLET FLY-CAP (*Amanita muscaria*). This fungus of birch woods contains several poisons which may cause drowsiness, excitement, paralysis or death. In many northern countries it has been utilised as a powerful intoxicant in drinks. It can be used, steeped in milk, for stupefying flies.

84

86. GOLDEN EAR (*Otidea onotica*). Most of the larger fleshy cup-fungi appearing on the ground in woods in autumn are brown in colour and broadly rounded in shape. In this species, which can be found in clusters among fallen oak leaves, the cups are split down one side and ear-shaped. Some specimens are as much as 10 cm (4 in.) high. The orange colour is sometimes flushed with pink as in a ripe peach. It is commonest under oak and hazel.

87. BIRD'S-NEST FUNGUS (*Cyathus striatus*). In these strange little fungi which grow on rotten sticks and matted leaves in woods, the egg-like peridioles are at first hidden by a skin which ruptures when the cups expand. They are attached by coiled threads and when the cups fill with water in wet weather, they become coated with mucilage and often jump out when splashed. Some are dispersed by sticking to passing animals.

Moors and Heaths

Many of the flowers of heaths and moorlands come into bloom quite late in the summer and continue to give rich colour to these open stretches of the countryside until well into the autumn. Some species, in fact, only reach perfection in September, notably the dwarf kinds of gorse, devil's-bit scabious and grass of Parnassus. Autumn rains refresh bright-green cushions of bog moss in the hollows as heather bells and bracken acquire rusty tints in contrast. A few butterflies linger for a while and the dark, velvety, orange-ringed caterpillars of the fox moth are conspicuous on the heather. High moors are deserted by most of their breeding birds but are still haunted by the native grouse, meadow pipits and skylarks, while siskins flock to seeding catkins on scattered birches. Red deer move down from the hills to the lower slopes at winter's approach.

88. RED GROUSE (*Lagopus scoticus*). Essentially birds of heather-clad, drier parts of moorlands, these grouse feed chiefly on the young shoots of heather, although in autumn they pick up seeds and berries to some extent. Much of their time is spent in cover, but when alarmed, they rise with a whirr of wings, calling 'go-back, go-back' as they skim away at speed and presently swoop to earth at a safe distance. Some move to lower moors as the weather gets colder.

89. SISKIN (*Carduelis spinus*). In autumn many of these small finches leave their breeding-haunts in northern pine woods to wander south in nomadic flocks and for several months they are to be seen feeding on the seeds of alder and birch in heathy and boggy country. In recent years they have also become resident in many English counties and now quite frequently visit bird-tables in our gardens where they appear as acrobatic as titmice.

90. SKYLARK (*Alauda arvensis*). The skylark is essentially a bird of open spaces, frequenting marsh pastures near the coast, chalk downs, heaths and moors at all seasons. In autumn the population is increased through the arrival of migrants from northern Europe and in suitable areas on calm, sunny days, they rise and sing almost as vigorously as in spring. They feed chiefly on seeds and green shoots.

91. GATEKEEPER or HEDGE BROWN (*Pyronia tithonus*). Usually a common single-brooded summer butterfly of hedgerows and grassy heaths in our coastal regions, this species often remains on the wing until well into September and is a frequent visitor to the blossoms of blackberry and knapweed. It is one of the very few butterflies which can be seen flying on dull days and even when light rain is falling. The caterpillars feed on grasses.

92. GRAYLING (*Hipparchia semele*). This species is widespread on the stony and sandy ground of hillsides, downland, heaths and dunes. Individuals tend to remain in one small area which they select as their special territory, but they may be carried far from home occasionally by strong winds. On settling, always with wings closed, they are well camouflaged by their mottled pattern and usually luff to one side to eliminate shadow.

91

92

93

93. SMALL COPPER (*Lycaena phlaeas*). This small, lively butterfly glitters with a fiery brilliance. It frequents many kinds of open country almost throughout Britain, but breeds only where sorrels are present as food for its downy, slug-shaped, green caterpillars. On sandy heaths it is associated with sheep's sorrel. Normally three broods are produced, the first in spring and the last in autumn. September females often have pronounced blue wing-crescents.

94. CATERPILLAR OF FOX MOTH (*Macrothylacia rubi*). In summer it is common to see rust-coloured male fox moths flying boldly and swiftly over heaths and moors, the females being active only at night. Eggs are laid chiefly on heather and the caterpillars become conspicuous as they perch fully exposed on their food-plants or sun themselves on rocks and grass. They are softly furry and black, with some brown hairs and yellow rings.

95

95. BELL HEATHER (*Erica cinerea*). The rich purple of this strictly west European heather dominates large areas of our drier and more acid sandy heathlands in August and September. On hot days the flowers have a honey-like fragrance which attracts bees and butterflies. In dry weather the bells produce a crisp, almost tinkling sound as one brushes through their ranks. Plants with pale purple or even pure-white flowers turn up occasionally.

96. CROSS-LEAVED HEATH (*Erica tetralix*). A long-flowering plant characteristic of bogs and wet heaths, it has downy, grey-green leaves arranged in whorls of four. The flowers are typically rosy, but white ones are not uncommon. They have narrow mouths and can be entered by some small insects, but are mostly self-pollinated. This heather often survives burning.

97. CROWBERRY (*Empetrum nigrum*). This heather-like shrub frequents peaty and sandy soils of moors and mountains, chiefly in the north. The narrow leaves have white slits showing beneath. Small male and female flowers appear on separate bushes in early spring and are succeeded by black fruits attractive to moorland birds. The foliage is fragrant like bog myrtle.

98. GRASS OF PARNASSUS (*Parnassia palustris*). The lily-like, ivory-white blossoms of this plant appear with startling effect in wet, peaty places at the beginning of autumn. They have tall, smooth stalks and pointed, heart-shaped leaves. As in saxifrages, the stamens bend over one by one to shed pollen on the stigmas. Small seeds pack the rounded capsules.

99. SOUTHERN DWARF GORSE (*Ulex nana*). This abounds on old heathlands in south-east England, but is absent from the north and west of Britain and from Ireland. It is generally smaller and less prickly than the more widespread *U. gallii* and has downy and usually light green branches. The flowers are typically lemon-coloured, with standards less than 12 mm (0·5 in.) long.

100. HAREBELL (*Campanula rotundifolia*). This slender perennial, known in Scotland as the 'bluebell', grows commonly in dry, acid grassland on sandy soils almost throughout Britain. The basal leaves are rounded and those on the flower stalks narrow and grass-like. The delicate, scentless flowers can be found from July until late September. They attract bees and butterflies.

99

100

101. GOLDEN-ROD (*Solidago virgaurea*). Our one wild species of golden-rod seldom grows above 60 cm (2 ft) high. Its brilliant yellow flowers are at their best in September, tufting heathy slopes and banks, various rocky places and dry, lightly shaded parts of woodlands. It has a wide distribution.

102. EARTH-BALL (*Scleroderma aurantium*). This is our commonest earth-ball growing on sandy heaths and in birch woods. It may be creamy or tinged with yellow and has conspicuous brownish scales. These fungi resemble truffles in their solid flesh and are sometimes used as an inferior substitute.

103. SPINY PUFFBALL (*Lycoperdon foetidum*). Many kinds of puffball appear on heaths and grassland in late summer and autumn, including a giant species whose flesh is edible when young. The ripe fungi hold masses of dark powdery spores which puff out when the receptacles are hit by rain-drops.

02

03

104. SICKENER (*Russula emetica*). Various species of *Russula* are common in our woodlands, their colours ranging through all the tints of the rainbow. They are rigid fungi with thick stalks and white or creamy gills and spores, and being somewhat brittle, the flesh is easily broken. Though not strictly poisonous, many have a nauseous peppery taste. This applies very noticeably to the sickener, so-called because it tends to cause vomiting if eaten in a raw state. It is one of several scarlet-capped species, and is generally associated with birches on heathy ground. Two very similar kinds grow under oaks and beeches.

105. CHANTERELLE (*Cantharellus cibarius*). This elegant egg-yellow fungus abounds on heathy banks, sometimes nested in moss; also where gorse and bracken have been burnt some months earlier. Though widespread in England, it is seen most commonly in the Scottish glens in late summer and autumn. A delicious edible species, it has firm flesh and a distinctive odour of apricots; it is also nutritious and rich in vitamins, with carotene giving it its distinctive colour. Care must be taken not to confuse it with the poisonous false chanterelle (*Hygrophoropsis aurantiaca*), a more 'papery' fungus with orange gills, growing under pines.

105

106. SLIMY LEOTIA (*Leotia lubrica*). A fleshy relative of the fungi known as 'earth-tongues' and producing spores in tubular sacs (asci) instead of on gills, this species appears in groups on moist, mossy banks of heaths, often with bracken, from August to October. It is found in such habitats throughout Britain. The fruit-bodies are only up to 6 cm (a little over 2 in.) high, with yellowish, granular stalks and gelatinous, honey-yellow or olive-green heads which become very slimy in wet weather. There is one other British species, the rarer *L. atrovirens*, which is entirely dark blue-green, to be found chiefly in moist, mossy woods.